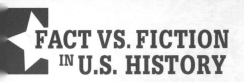

FACT VS. FICTION
IN U.S. HISTORY

THOMAS
EDISON

AND THE INVENTION
OF THE LIGHT BULB:
SEPARATING FACT FROM FICTION

by Megan Cooley Peterson

CAPSTONE PRESS
a capstone imprint

Published by Capstone Press, an imprint of Capstone
1710 Roe Crest Drive, North Mankato, Minnesota 56003
capstonepub.com

Library of Congress Cataloging-in-Publication Data
is available on the Library of Congress website.
ISBN: 9781666339710 (library binding)
ISBN: 9781666339727 (paperback)
ISBN: 9781666339734 (ebook PDF)

Summary: Thomas Edison was a famous American inventor in the late 1800s. Over time, many stories were told about his work, especially about how he invented the light bulb. But this isn't true! Discover what's fact and what's fiction in the story of Thomas Edison and his role in the invention of the light bulb.

Editorial Credits
Editor: Carrie Sheely; Designer: Bobbie Nuytten; Media Researcher: Donna Metcalf; Production Specialist: Whitney Schaefer

Image Credits
Alamy: Historic Collection, 25; Getty Images: Bettmann, 20, Boyer/Roger Viollet, 28, Fox Photos, 15, 23, Hulton Archive, 17, Jeff Greenberg, front cover (bottom), Keystone, 5, back cover (middle right), Oxford Science Archive, 7, Schenectady Museum Association, 16, 18, 19, Science & Society Picture Library, 11, 21, 24, 27, Stock Montage, 6, ullstein bild Dtl., 22, Universal History Archive, 10, Universal Images Group, 8, 13; Shutterstock: Everett Collection, front cover (top)

Source Notes
Page 18, "I have it now!" Mark Aldrich, "Edison's Happy New Year," The Gad About Town, December 31, 2014, https://thegadabouttown.com/2014/12/31/edisons-happy-new-year/, Accessed February 2022.

All internet sites appearing in back matter were available and accurate when this book was sent to press.

Table of Contents

Words in **bold** are in the glossary.

Introduction

It was New Year's Eve in 1879. Many people around the world were celebrating a new year. Inventor Thomas Edison had plans to celebrate his new light bulb. Edison had been working on an **incandescent** bulb for more than a year. That night, he invited the public to view his creation at his laboratory. He wanted to put on a show never seen before—dozens of light bulbs powered by electricity.

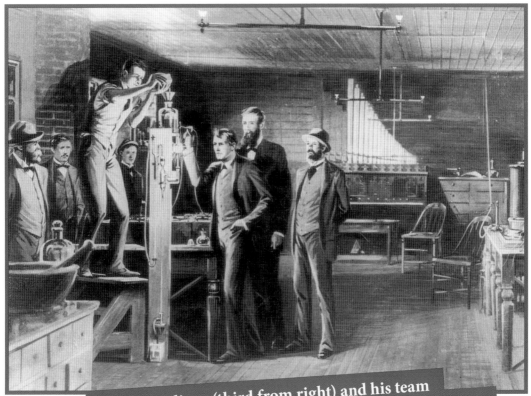

Thomas Edison (third from right) and his team successfully created a long-lasting light bulb in October 1879.

Many people believe that Thomas Edison invented the light bulb. They think he was the first to dream up electric lights. But this story isn't completely true. Edison wasn't the only inventor working on the light bulb. He wasn't even the first. Read on and find out what really happened.

Chapter One

Early Electric Lights

One of the biggest **myths** about the light bulb is that Thomas Edison created it all by himself. But Edison wasn't the first inventor interested in electric lights. In fact, he wasn't even born when the first electric lights were made.

In the early 1800s, Humphry Davy invented the arc light. His light used two carbon rods. Electricity flowed easily through the carbon. A **current** jumped from one rod to the other. The current made a small arc, which gave off a lot of light. Davy showed off his new device at the Royal Society in Great Britain around 1810.

Humphry Davy

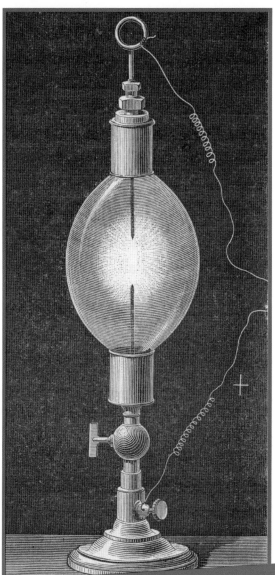

Davy's arc light was very bright, but it didn't last very long.

⭐ Fact!

Edison was born on February 11, 1847. That's almost 40 years after Davy invented the arc light.

Let it Glow

Davy's new lights soon lit up locations across Europe. They were installed in factories, railway stations, and even ships. These bright lights made dark spaces safer to work in. But they had limits. Arc lighting was too bright for small spaces, such as in people's homes. The arc light's rods also lasted only a few hours.

Arc lights were useful for lighting up city streets.

Davy experimented with another kind of lighting—incandescent light. He ran a current through a **platinum** wire. As the wire heated up, it began to glow. It wasn't as bright as arc lighting. It was easier to look at. But Davy had a problem. His new bulb needed a huge battery to power it. These batteries cost a lot of money. People couldn't afford them. Davy's bulb wouldn't work for everyday life. But many historians say Davy is the creator of the first incandescent bulb.

Fact!

Today, people use arc lights in searchlights, floodlights, and other lights that need to be very bright.

New Power Source

Charles Brush

American inventor Charles Brush improved the arc light in the 1870s. His light didn't burn out as quickly. He also perfected a machine called a **dynamo** to power the light. This machine makes electricity using fast-spinning magnets. The dynamo was much cheaper than batteries.

In April 1879, several of Brush's arc lights lit up a park in downtown Cleveland, Ohio. His lights had carbon rods housed in glass orbs. They sat on tall posts. Soon, Brush's arc lights could be found in many U.S. cities.

★ Fact!

Brush lit up Niagara Falls on July 4, 1879, with 16 arc lights. At the time, one newspaper mistakenly gave Thomas Edison the credit for the event.

This new outdoor lighting amazed most people.
But when the arc lights were moved indoors, the
excitement stopped. The lights made a loud humming
noise, like a swarm of bees. They also gave rooms a
strange blue color. The race to invent an indoor bulb
for everyday use was on.

Brush's improved arc lights helped light
up many city streets at night.

Chapter Two

Moving Light Indoors

Davy's incandescent bulb inspired many inventors. In the 1840s, American J. W. Starr made a bulb using carbon and platinum **filaments**. But dynamos hadn't been invented yet. Starr faced the same problem Davy had—he had to use expensive batteries.

Around this time, Frederick de Moleyns was working on his own bulb. In 1841, he received a British **patent** for his design. This was the first patent for an incandescent bulb. It wouldn't be the last.

When he created it, Humphry Davy's battery was the world's biggest source of electrical power.

The batteries used for the first incandescent light bulbs were big and expensive. They were not useful for most people.

In 1859, American Moses Farmer created bulbs that could stay lit for an entire month. These small bulbs were powered by batteries. But Farmer found that running the bulbs cost too much money. It was cheaper to burn gas or oil to make light.

Across the Atlantic

In England, Joseph W. Swan began experimenting with bulbs as early as 1848. By 1860, he had created a bulb that used carbon paper filaments. But he couldn't keep enough air out of the glass bulb. The air made his bulb burn out quickly. Swan set his bulb aside. He chose not to get a patent for his early ideas. This choice would directly affect Edison in the years to come.

Joseph Swan

Chapter Three

The Wizard of Menlo Park

By the summer of 1878, Thomas Edison was one of the world's most successful inventors. He had already made improvements to the **telegraph** to allow people to communicate over long distances. He soon turned to the light bulb. He wondered how he could improve the bulb. He wanted it to last longer and be cheaper to use.

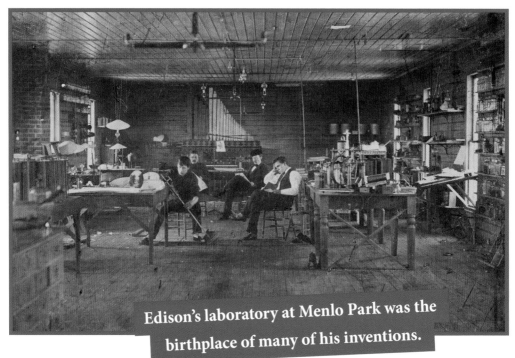

Edison's laboratory at Menlo Park was the birthplace of many of his inventions.

Edison had a head start over other inventors. He could study previous bulbs to see what worked and what didn't. Edison also had a laboratory in Menlo Park, New Jersey. He hired skilled assistants to help him. The lab had a vacuum pump. It could remove air from glass bulbs. No air meant bulbs could burn a lot longer.

EDISON'S FAVORITE INVENTION

Thomas Edison was always coming up with new ideas. His favorite invention was the **phonograph**. This device recorded sound and played it back. The first words he recorded were "Mary had a little lamb."

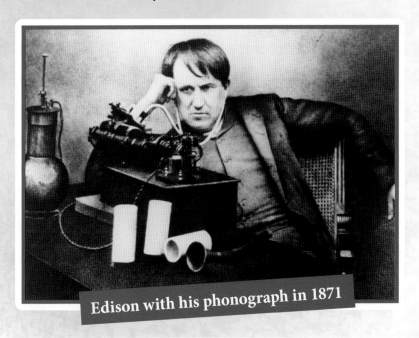

Edison with his phonograph in 1871

Big Goals

Edison needed a way to power his bulb. He bought a dynamo from Moses Farmer and William Wallace. He made improvements so it worked even better. The dynamo gave him a new goal. He wanted to create a system that could light up several city blocks. Edison planned to bury copper wires that would carry electricity to each house. His new system would replace gas lighting, which burned fuel to make a flame.

Edison was excited by his ideas. He imagined the end result of a city lit up with electric lights. He soon told a reporter, "I have it now!" But there was one problem—he didn't have a bulb yet!

However, Edison was eager to bring lights to the city. Even with no proof of success, Edison easily raised money. Wealthy businessmen such as J. P. Morgan and the Vanderbilts believed Edison could do it. They helped fund his work. In 1878, the Edison Electric Light Company was born.

J. P. Morgan

With the help of his investors, Edison opened the Edison Electric Light Company in 1878.

Edison's First Bulbs

In early October 1878, Edison made his first bulb. He used a platinum filament. He also created a device to control the temperature of the current. That way the filament wouldn't burn up so fast. Still, this bulb only lasted 40 minutes. Edison tossed out his idea and tried something new.

At the Menlo Park lab, Edison and his team tried thousands of different filaments before finding one that lasted a long time.

In October 1879, Edison tried to make a carbon filament. He and his team used thin filaments that used less current. They experimented with filaments made from materials such as cotton thread and beard hair. They eventually used tiny loops of **carbonized** cardboard. This new bulb lasted almost 14 hours before burning out.

For the 1879 New Year's Eve demonstration, about 50 of Edison's bulbs lit up Menlo Park. A glassblower made each bulb by hand. The show was a huge success. People came from all over to see Edison's electric lights.

Edison's carbon filament light bulb

Fact!

Menlo Park became known as the Village of Light.

Chapter Four

Battle of the Bulbs

Word of Edison's New Year's Eve light show spread quickly. British newspapers soon reminded the world of Joseph Swan. He had continued to work on his light bulb. Swan had given a show of his bulb to the Newcastle Chemical Society in early 1879. This was months before Edison. But Swan's bulb used a carbon rod that burned out quickly. It also coated the inside of the bulb with soot. He later switched to a cotton filament.

Swan continued his experiments with light bulbs in the mid-1870s after better vacuum pumps became available.

Fact!

In 1879, Mosley Street in England became the world's first public street to be lit by incandescent light bulbs.

Edison and Swan weren't the only inventors battling to make the best bulb. Americans William Sawyer and Hiram Maxim also found some success. But Sawyer's filament broke easily. Maxim's bulb gave off a pulsing light. Edison still had a chance to make the first useful, affordable indoor light bulb.

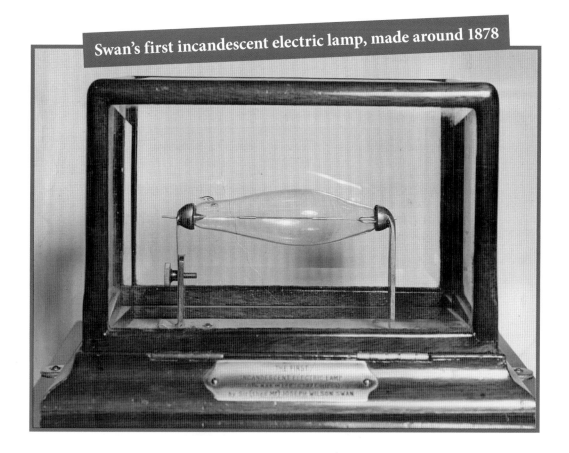

Swan's first incandescent electric lamp, made around 1878

Finding the Right Filament

Edison and his team needed to find a filament that would last longer. Edison was sure a natural **fiber** would work best. They tested everything from horsehair to silk. In the end, they tested around 6,000 types of fibers. They chose Japanese bamboo. These bulbs could stay lit up to about 1,000 hours. Edison's bulb was ready to be sold to customers.

Fact!

Edison and Swan's bulbs were called Ediswans.

Patent Wars

In January 1880, Edison was granted a U.S. patent for his bulb. It protected his ideas. The Edison company then began a legal case against Swan in England. Edison wanted to control the light bulb market there. However, lawyers for both sides knew Swan had a strong case. Swan could prove he'd worked on his bulb longer than Edison. They decided to work together instead. In 1883, the inventors formed the successful Edison and Swan United Electric Light Company.

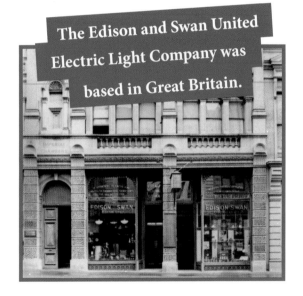

The Edison and Swan United Electric Light Company was based in Great Britain.

TOP PRIZE

In 1881, Edison displayed his lighting system at the International Exposition of Electricity in Paris. Other inventors, including Swan, showed off their lights as well. Edison's lights won the top prize. Swan sent Edison a message to congratulate him.

Chapter Five

Lighting a City

Edison didn't invent the light bulb. But he was the first to create a system to deliver electricity to power his bulbs. In 1882, he opened the first electrical power station in the United States. The Pearl Street Station in New York lit up 1 square mile (2.6 square kilometers) of homes and buildings in Lower Manhattan. Edison built six huge dynamos to power the station. They were nicknamed "Jumbos." The dynamos created direct current, or DC. This system could deliver electricity only over short distances. An underground system delivered the electricity directly to homes through copper wires.

Fact!

Alternating current, or AC, is used most often today. AC can travel much farther than DC.

Several steam-powered dynamo machines at Pearl Street Station produced electricity for Edison's light bulbs.

The *New York Times* building was one of the first to glow with Edison's bulbs. Soon, Edison power plants were lighting cities around the United States. Residents in Laramie, Wyoming, celebrated their new Edison power station in 1886 with a concert and fireworks. Indoor electric lighting was here to stay.

The idea that Thomas Edison invented the light bulb has been around for more than 100 years. But it's not true. In fact, no single person invented the light bulb. Like most inventions, many people helped to develop it. Edison built upon the work of others. Most historians agree that Edison did make the world's first useful light bulb. He also created the world's first power station.

Edison with his incandescent light bulb in the early 1880s

Technology for light bulbs continued to change. Inventors came up with new ideas. Today, many people use LED light bulbs in their homes. LEDs last longer than incandescent bulbs and give off better light. Still, Edison's work helped make electric lighting possible.

The Mythology of Thomas Edison and the Invention of the Light Bulb

Fiction Thomas Edison invented the world's first light bulb.

Fact Inventors had experimented with light bulbs since the early 1800s. Humphry Davy created the world's first incandescent bulb before Edison was born.

Fiction Edison patented the first incandescent light bulb.

Fact In 1841, Frederick de Moleyns received the first patent for an incandescent light bulb. Other inventors patented bulbs at about the same time as Edison's.

Fiction Edison's light bulb was completely original.

Fact Edison did not come up with his light bulb design on his own. Instead, he improved on previous light bulbs. He also worked with a large team of skilled assistants.

Glossary

carbonize (KAR-buh-nyz)—to heat a natural fiber at a high temperature until it turns to pure carbon

current (KUHR-uhnt)—the flow of electrons

dynamo (DYE-nuh-moh)—a generator that produces electricity by turning a magnet inside a coil of wire

fiber (FY-buhr)—a long, thin thread of material

filament (FI-luh-muhnt)—a thin fiber or wire that is heated electrically to produce light

incandescent (in-kuhn-DEH-suhnt)—producing light after being heated to a high temperature

myth (MITH)—a false idea that many people believe

patent (PAH-tuhnt)—a legal document giving someone the sole right to make, use, or sell an invention for a certain number of years

phonograph (FOH-nuh-graf)—a device that plays recorded sounds recorded on a revolving cylinder or disk; also called a record player

platinum (PLAH-tuh-nuhm)—a silver-white metal

telegraph (TEH-luh-graf)—a machine that uses electrical signals to send messages over long distances

Read More

Gagne, Tammy. *Fact and Fiction of American Invention.* Minneapolis: Abdo Publishing, 2022.

Proudfit, Benjamin. *Thomas Edison and the Light Bulb.* New York: Gareth Stevens Publishing, 2023.

Yasuda, Anita. *Thomas Edison.* New York: Lightbox Learning, 2023.

Internet Sites

DK Findout!: Light Bulb
dkfindout.com/us/science/amazing-inventions/light-bulb/

Ducksters: Biography of Thomas Edison
ducksters.com/biography/thomas_edison.php

Smithsonian: Edison Light Bulb
si.edu/newsdesk/snapshot/edison-light-bulb

Index

About the Author

Megan Cooley Peterson is a children's book author and editor. Her book *How To Build Hair-Raising Haunted Houses* (Capstone Press, 2011) was selected as a Book of Note by the TriState Young Adult Review Committee. When not writing, Megan enjoys movies, books, and all things Halloween. She lives in Minnesota with her husband and daughter.